A N Pearson

Report

on the suitability of the River Yarra for the irrigation of the Botanical

Gardens

A N Pearson

Report
on the suitability of the River Yarra for the irrigation of the Botanical Gardens

ISBN/EAN: 9783744650632

Printed in Europe, USA, Canada, Australia, Japan

Cover: Foto ©ninafisch / pixelio.de

More available books at **www.hansebooks.com**

1890.

VICTORIA.

REPORT

ON THE

SUITABILITY OF THE RIVER YARRA FOR THE IRRIGATION OF THE BOTANICAL GARDENS,

BY

MESSRS. C. R. BLACKETT AND A. N. PEARSON.

PRESENTED TO BOTH HOUSES OF PARLIAMENT BY HIS EXCELLENCY'S COMMAND.

By Authority:
ROBT, S. BRAIN, GOVERNMENT PRINTER, MELBOURNE.

No. 91.—[1s.]—3835.

APPROXIMATE COST OF REPORT.

Preparation—Not given.
Printing (760 copies) :¶   ..   £ s. d.
                                                 27 13 6

REPORT

BY MESSRS. C. R. BLACKETT AND A. N. PEARSON ON THE SUITABILITY OF THE RIVER YARRA FOR THE IRRIGATION OF THE BOTANICAL GARDENS.

DEPARTMENT OF AGRICULTURE,
Agricultural Laboratory, 17A and 19A Queen-street,
Melbourne, 16th April, 1890.

SIR,

We have the honour to report that, acting on instructions received conformably with your memorandum, No. O.89/16289, of the 27th August, 1889, to the Honorable the Minister of Mines, we have undertaken and completed a critical examination of the river Yarra, with a view to ascertaining if the water of that river taken from the surface only, anywhere near the present pumping station, could be used for irrigating the Botanical Gardens.

Our instructions were received on the 31st August, 1889, and we immediately placed ourselves in communication with Mr. Guilfoyle, the Director of the Botanic and Domain Gardens. This gentleman stated that at that time there was no trouble with the water obtained at the pumping station, there being then a rapid current of fresh water due to recent rains, and that it was only between the 1st October and the 31st March that danger from the saltness of the river was to be apprehended. He promised to let us have the earliest intimation of the water becoming too salt. We thereupon wrote to you on the 5th September, 1889, stating that we could not for the reasons mentioned commence our examination until some time in the month of October; we also mentioned that it would be necessary to gather samples of the water systematically for a month or two, and that we purposed paying special attention to the difference in the quality of the water at different depths, at different positions up the river, at different tidal periods, and at night and day.

No report reached us from the Botanic Gardens as to the saltness of the river during the months of September and October, and on the 11th November we again communicated with the director on the subject, receiving reply that the water was still fresh, as shown by a crude test which was being applied at the pumping station, a test, namely, as to its readiness to produce lather with soap. On the 11th December we sent down and obtained a sample from the well which receives the river water at the pumping station. This sample, on analysis, was found to contain 67 parts of chlorine (representing 110·4 parts of salt) per 100,000. We were informed that this was the first day on which the river had shown indications of being injuriously salt, and we decided to commence the examination forthwith.

Before beginning operations it was necessary to decide upon the limit of saltness which could be safely allowed in water intended for irrigating the Botanic Gardens. It was hoped that this question would have been settled by direct experiment, but the experiments commenced to this end in the small conservatory attached to the Agricultural Laboratory were stopped through damage done to the experimental plants by mice, and, as it was too late in the season to begin the work over again, the experiments had to be put off until next season. A limit may, however, be fixed by indirect methods. Thus, an outside dressing of salt in ordinary farming is 5 cwt. per acre, and this amount should not be given often unless there be a heavy rainfall and free drainage, so as to allow the soil to be properly washed. Suppose, now, a water to contain 50 parts of salt per 100,000, then soil irrigated with 1 in. depth of such water would receive 1 cwt. of salt per acre, and irrigated with 10 in. depth of such water it would receive half-a-ton of salt per acre, which, as we have seen, is an excessive amount.

A 2

4

Of course all plants are not equally affected by salt. Salsolaceous and many coast plants seem to be benefited by comparatively excessive amounts, while others, such as ferns, are very sensitive to its action, and suffer with a slight excess.

It is convenient, as saving the labour of calculation, to represent the salt by the amount of chlorine it contains. Salt consists of 35·5 parts by weight of chlorine, and 23 parts of sodium; and, in examining the water for salt, the most expeditious method is to estimate simply the chlorine in it, and to take this chlorine as an index of the amount of salt; thus, 30 parts of chlorine per 100,000 would indicate approximately 50 parts of salt per 100,000. In this report the results of analysis are entered simply as chlorine in parts per 100,000.

And judging from the considerations above given as to the amount of salt used in ordinary farming, we may say that a water containing, as a usual thing, 15 parts of chlorine per 100,000 may be safely used for irrigation; that an average of 30 parts of chlorine per 100,000 is an outside limit for an open sandy or gravelly soil, where there is sufficient winter rain to wash away the salt which may accumulate during the summer; and that 50 parts of chlorine per 100,000 is the outside limit permissible, and that this amount should occur only occasionally.

This point being decided, our attention was next given to the vertical distribution of salt in the river, so that we might be able to advise upon the possibility of obtaining sufficiently fresh water by taking from the surface only. For the purpose of this investigation it was not sufficient to take samples from only one point in the river, as for instance from mid-stream, since the conditions might be different near the bank; nor was it sufficient to take samples simply from the top and the bottom; for in case the water at the surface was found to be fresh and at the bottom salt, it would be necessary to ascertain to what depth the fresh water extended. It was necessary also to consider the possibility of local currents and eddies which might at times and in places carry with them streams of salt close up to the surface. And, finally, it was necessary to consider how far the vertical distribution of salt in the river might be affected by tides and by falls of rain.

In order that all these points might be properly tested, it was necessary to take samples in such a way as to represent complete sections of the river; these sections to be taken periodically, at intervals to be decided by experience. It was decided first of all to take them on certain days at intervals of a week, and on each of these days to take them twice, namely, at high and at low tides.

Description of Gathering Samples.—For this purpose a rope long enough to stretch across the river was obtained, and divided, by convenient marks, into regular intervals. This being stretched across the river enabled those in charge of the boat to quickly fix themselves at the proper horizontal distances. For fixing upon the points in vertical depth, two light iron gas-pipes were obtained, a shorter and a longer one, to be used respectively for shallow and great depths. These were graduated into 6-in. intervals. A case for containing the bottle was screwed on to one end of the pipes. A simple arrangement was clamped on to the side of the boat, allowing the rod to be let down into the water through a vertical groove; by this means the rod was easily held in a vertical position. The operation of gathering samples will be readily understood from the accompanying sketch.

At the time of gathering samples by aid of the rope, two men were employed, one standing 100 yards above and the other 100 yards below the site, so as to warn boats to look out for the rope.

It was not considered necessary for the purposes of this investigation to go deeper than 15 feet. The depths at first decided upon were as follows:—

At A, Mid-stream.	At B and B', About 10 feet from A.	At C and C', About 1½ feet from Bank.	At D and D', 3 feet from Bank.
Surface	Surface	Surface	Surface
6 inches deep	6 inches deep	1 foot deep	1 foot
1 foot „	1 foot „	2 feet „	Bottom
2 feet „	2 feet „	3 „ „	
3 „ „	3 „ „	Bottom	
5 „ „	5 „ „		
10 „ „	10 „ „		
15 „ „			

The bottles, in addition to having been marked by means of a diamond, were arranged in proper order in a case with divisions in it; thus the possibility of error owing to the accidental mixing of the bottles was minimised. The bottles having been let down in the water to the proper depth, the india-rubber stopper was drawn by means of a string; the bottle was kept in its position until no more bubbles of air rose from it; it was then drawn up and replaced by an empty one. In this way it required from 35 to 45 minutes to gather the 38 samples representing one section.

The sites selected for these sections were those marked 1, 2, and 3 in the accompanying sketch map, namely, at the present pumping house, near the old pumping house, and a little below the Botanic Gardens footbridge.

Preliminary Examination.—Preliminary samples were taken on the 16th December, at high and at low tide, at the present pumping station (No. 1), in mid-stream and about 13 feet from the left (south) bank. The results are given in Table I. It will be seen that the chlorine was in all cases above 30 parts per 100,000; that is to say, outside the limit which we had fixed upon as a safe average. It was considerably above that limit at a depth of 10 feet. In mid-stream, at shallow depths, it was a little less at high tide than at low, whereas at a depth of 10 feet it was considerably less at low than at high tide—a fact which seems to indicate that with the ebbing tide the briny under-current was drawn out to sea, and the fresh upper-current, by the commotion thus caused, became to a certain extent mixed with the under-current, and thus rendered salter. Near the bank, however, the water at shallow depths was less salt at low tide than at high, an irregularity similar to many others which were subsequently observed. Preliminary samples were again taken on the 18th December at high tide, and throughout indicated that the water was getting salter; at a depth of 10 feet the water had already risen to 711 parts per 100,000.

The first complete sections were taken on 24th December, and the results are given on Tables I., II., and III. From the 21st to 23rd December heavy rain had fallen, and it was anticipated that the water would be less salt than before; nevertheless, the results gained were very surprising, for they showed that at all the three sections the water was absolutely fresh down to the lowest depths. They demonstrated how rapidly at this early stage in the season the river could be swept clean by flood waters.

Four days after this, namely, on the 28th, a sample was taken from the pumping house well, and showed that the chlorine had already risen to 30·6 parts per 100,000. On the 30th December it was only 20·6, and on the 31st again 30·6.

On the 2nd January the second complete sections were taken, but this time from only one site, namely, the present pumping station, since the taking of three sections had been found during the first trial to absorb more time than could be spared.

Vertical Distribution.—The results gained this time were interesting and instructive. They showed (*vide* Table I., 2nd January, low tide) that, whereas in mid-stream the chlorine was only 32·5, at the banks it averaged 50. Indeed, the fresh water current seemed to be concentrated within a breadth of 20 feet in the middle of the river. They also showed that at shallow depths the water was salter on the left side of the stream than on the right, though not very much so, the figures being 51 on the left and 48·6 on the right. They showed that at a depth of 1 foot the water began to increase in saltness. They also showed the existence of minor local currents producing considerable irregularities in the distribution of the salt; for, whereas at the bottom (about 8 feet deep) at C, 13 feet off the right bank, the chlorine was 840; at C¹, the corresponding position on the left side of the river, it was less, viz., 592; but at B, midway between A and C¹ on the right side, and at B¹, the corresponding position on the left side, the conditions were reversed, being less, viz., 766, on the right, and more, viz., 920, on the left side. All these results were in the main confirmed by the section taken on the same day at high tide, as also by subsequent sections both here and at other sites (*vide* Table I., 9th, 16th, 23rd, and 30th January and 6th February; also Table II.; also Table III., especially 16th, 23rd, and 30th January and 6th February). It was to be anticipated, however, that the local currents would not be constant, and subsequent observations showed them to be always changing their position. But the point of practical importance was that they did not in any marked manner affect the distribution of salt at the surface.

Influence of Tides.—It was expected that the saltness of the water would vary with the tide, and it seemed not improbable that, in case the river might be excessively salt with one tide, sufficiently fresh water might be obtained by pumping only during the alternate tides. As to which tide would produce the greater saltness it was not easy to surmise beforehand. At certain positions in the river the incoming tide would, by bringing in a current of salt water, possibly increase the surface saltness; at these positions the saltness would be greater at high tide and less at low tide. But at other portions of the river—probably, indeed, throughout its greater tidal length—the effect of the incoming tide would be to retard the outflowing current, thus damming back the fresh water on the surface of the river, and hence lessening the surface saltness. An inspection of the results given in Tables I.—V. will show that this latter was the case; with readily explainable exceptions, the water at the surface was less salt at high tides than at low. These exceptions, however, were not of such a kind that they could easily be foreseen; therefore, no simple rule for taking water only at high tide could be given. The average of a long period is, however, in favour of high tides. Thus, at the *Richmond Boat Sheds*, on the surface of the left bank (Table IV., D[1] surface) an average of fourteen days observations gave the following results :—

High tide ...   . 75·5 parts of chlorine per 100,000
Low tide ...   . 94·1   ,,   ,,   ,,

Difference between Night and Day.—It was not found possible, without considerably extra labour, to investigate this point.

Difference between Mid-stream and Sides.—This point has been already referred to under the head of "*Vertical Distribution;*" the observations made in the early stages of the investigation were fully confirmed by all the subsequent observations; and it was found that at all the stations, right up to the Twickenham Ferry, the water was fresher, often considerably so, in the middle of the river than near the banks.

Influence of Falls of Rain.—At the top of Tables I. and IV. are notes showing, on various days, the falls of rain at the Melbourne Observatory. These, of course, are not a direct indication of the rainfall over the whole basin of the Yarra; probably, whenever rain occurs at Melbourne, much heavier rain occurs on the mountains, in which are the chief sources of the Yarra.

The influence of heavy rain in the early part of the season is evinced very clearly by the observations taken on the 24th December, and already reverted to. A fall of 1·16 inches at Melbourne on the 21st to 23rd December was accompanied by a flooding and cleansing of the river throughout. By the 2nd January, however, the river at the pumping station was getting increasingly salt. But a very small shower of rain at Melbourne was accompanied by a considerable diminution in the saltness on the 9th; and the influence of heavy rain on the 11th was decidedly noticeable in the observations up to the 18th January. Again, about the 15th February (*vide* Tables I., IV., and V.), falls of 20 cents on the 14th and 17th were accompanied by a rapid drop in the saltness of the water. For instance, in the well, the chlorine dropped from about 150 on the 14th to 30 on the 17th; and, at *Richmond Boat Sheds*, it dropped from over 70 at high tide in mid-stream on the 14th to only 7 on the 17th. Falls of 20 cents and 15 cents on the 7th and 11th March were not accompanied by such marked diminution of the saltness : but whether this fact was due to the rainfall on the mountains at this time not having been so great, or to the increasing dryness and consequent absorptiveness of the soil in the Yarra basin after the hot weather— either of which causes would result in less fresh water flowing into the river—or whether it was due to the accumulation of salt at this time and its extension up the river, the observations taken do not enable us to decide. It is very likely, however, that the latter cause was a considerably operative one.

Gradual Extension of Salt up the River.—The observations up to 18th January did not give any decided indication that it would not be possible to get sufficiently fresh water from near the present pumping house. There was nothing to positively indicate the impracticability of obtaining good water by judiciously selecting for pumping only times of low saltness, and by the use of a floating rose, either near the left bank or in mid-stream at the Botanic Gardens footbridge (site No. 3). But on the 20th January the river began to get salter, and on the 24th January at the Botanic Gardens footbridge in mid-stream the chlorine at the surface was already 99. On the 22nd, therefore, observations were commenced at a new site—No. 4 on the accompanying sketch map. With the exception of two or three days, from 25th to 30th January, this did not seem an unpromising site; but for eleven days, from 5th to 15th February, the observations gave quite forbidding results. Consequently two new sites —Nos. 5 and 6 on the map—were taken up on 6th February. For two or three days these appeared promising; but on the 10th February it was found necessary to proceed to site No. 7, still further up the river; and on the 13th it was necessary to go again still higher (*vide* Tables IV. and V.). The site now fixed upon, namely No. 10, or "Toorak Bend," seemed perfectly safe; for from the 15th to the 26th February, although lower down the river the water was and had for some time been excessively salt, it was here no salter at the surface than it had, on the 10th, been found to be above and below Dight's Falls. This site then seemed absolutely safe. But on the 4th March the salt had crept up even to this place, and a new site still further on— No. 11, a little below Twickenham Ferry—was taken up. The water here was still considerably less salt than at Toorak Bend.

The heavy rains commenced at Melbourne on the 25th March, and on the 28th observations at all stations were stopped. They had for the sake of comparison been continued up to this date at the present pumping station (No. 1), at the Richmond boat sheds (No. 4), and at the South Yarra railway bridge (No. 6).

GENERAL CONCLUSIONS.

(*a*) *The Season Just Past.*—During the season just past, by omitting to take water on two or three days of excessive saltness, an abundant supply of fresh water suitable for irrigating the Botanic Gardens could have been obtained during the dry weather by fixing the intake at the site named in our map the "Toorak Bend;" such a supply could not have been obtained at any point lower down the river. By taking the water at the Twickenham Ferry, it is very probable (though the observations there do not extend far enough to make an absolute statement possible) that such a supply of water could have been obtained by pumping on all days and in all tides without exception.

(*b*) *Past and Previous Seasons.*— A general impression in regard to the season just past is, that it was as trying a one as is ever likely to occur; so that if the water has remained fresh at Twickenham this year, it is likely to do so in all years. We have, however (through the courtesy of Mr. Ellery, the Government Astronomer), been able to examine the rainfall records of all the past recorded years; the results are given in Tables VI. and VII. From Table VI. it will be seen that there have been several years of more prolonged drought than has occurred during the season just past; these periods are underlined in the Table. We would refer especially to the periods November, 1864, to April, 1865; February and March, 1870; and January to March, 1882.

It is not so much the action of the tides that must be considered as causing the salt to ascend the river, but the slow diffusion of the salt into the fresh water. This diffusion takes place mainly along the bed of the river and along the banks, and in a season of little rainfall the salt gradually creeps up the river for two or three miles above Prince's Bridge. The more copious the fresh water down-flow, the longer will it take for the salt to creep up. But if, owing to prolonged dry weather, the down current becomes contracted to a surface stream of shallow depth in the middle of the river, then the conditions are favorable to a rapid diffusion of the salt up the bed of the river. Hence in a period, for instance, like that of 1882, it is quite likely that the surface of the river at Twickenham Ferry would, towards the end of the season, exceed the safe limit. It is to be noted in Table VII., giving the daily rainfalls, that even in the previous year, 1889, there was from 8th February to 18th March, a longer period of light rainfall than we had this year between 11th January and 14th February.

There is also to be considered the possibility of the gradually saturation of the river bed with salt. Whether this will take place or not, and what, in case it should, would be the effect on the saltness of the water at the surface, we can do no more than surmise and not decide. But this is a contingency which should not be disregarded.

Final Conclusion.—Considering all these things, we are of opinion that some stage higher up than the Twickenham Ferry would be necessary in order to be within the limits of safety. Above this point there is an acute bend in the river, which results in a point more than 1½ miles higher up, measuring along the course of the stream, to be approximated to the point of the ferry, so as overland to be little more than quarter of a mile distant. We refer to the point crossed by the Hawthorn railway bridge. We feel confident in recommending this bridge as a perfectly safe place from which to draw the water by constant pumping for irrigating the Botanic Gardens.

As to the best means of conveying the water from this point, and as to what advantage, if any, would be gained, from an engineering point of view, by taking the water from here instead of from above Dight's Falls, it is not for us to say. The distance saved in a straight line would not be great; but it may be the engineering would be simpler.

There are still, however, two alternatives possible. The one is, to enlarge the reservoir at the Botanic Gardens, so as to make it capable of storing a six weeks' supply. If this were done the water could be taken in at a point of the river not far removed from the present pumping station. The other is to dam back the salt water by submerged flood-gates above the Prince's Bridge. As to which would be most feasible and economical, from an engineering point of view, we cannot say.

In conclusion we have to acknowledge that the main labour of gathering and testing the samples for the purpose of this investigation has devolved upon Mr. P. R. Scott, the water analysis assistant in the Agricultural Laboratory.

We have the honour to be, Sir,
Your most obedient servants,

C. R. BLACKETT,
Government Analyst.

A. N. PEARSON,
Government Agricultural Chemist.

A. W. HOWITT, Esq.,
Secretary for Mines.

Sketch Map
of the
RIVER YARRA
from Prince's Bridge to Yarra Bend

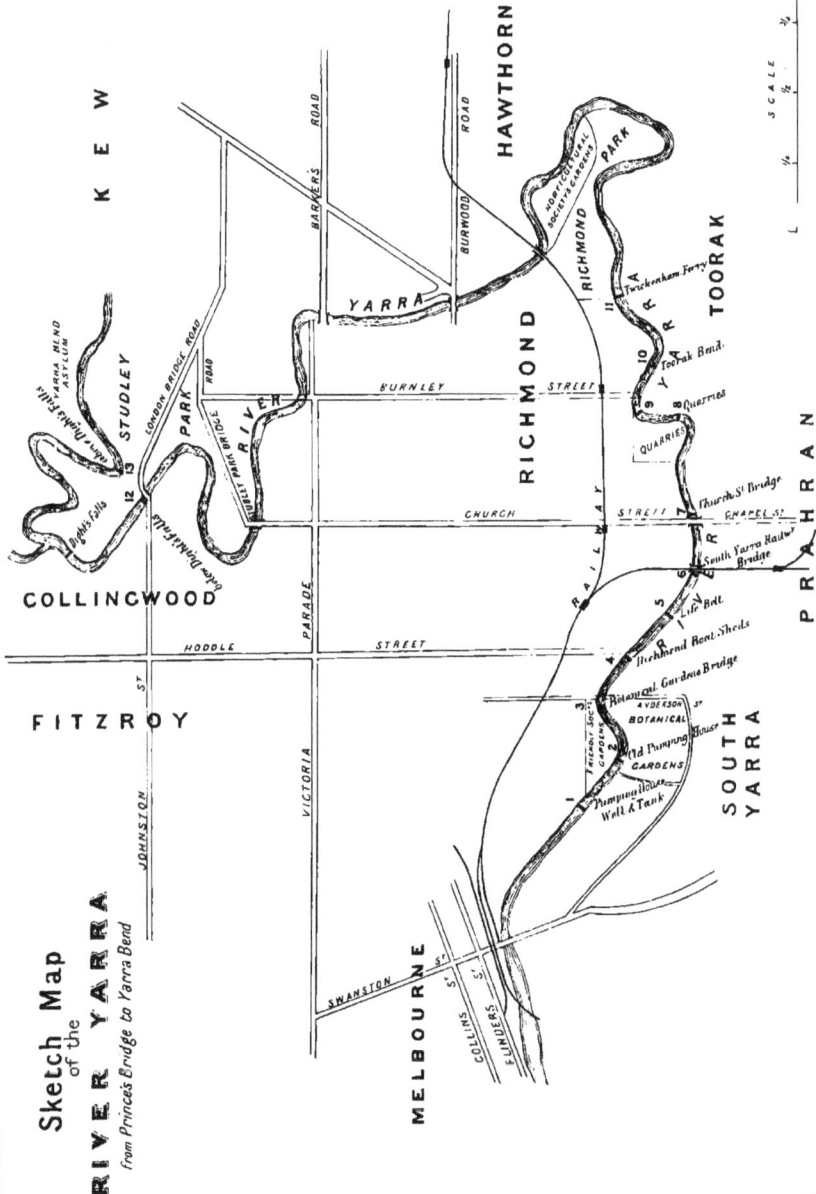

SCALE

1 Mile

KEW

HAWTHORN

TOORAK

RICHMOND PARK

HORTICULTURAL SOCIETY GROUNDS

Twickenham Ferry

Toorak Bend

Quarries

QUARRIES

YARRA

BURNLEY STREET

YARRA RIVER

Yarra Bend Asylum

Dights Falls

Yarra Bend Lunatic Asylum

STUDLEY PARK

LONDON BRIDGE ROAD

STUDLEY PARK ROAD

Studley Park Bridge

COLLINGWOOD

Upper Darling Rd

BARKERS ROAD

BURWOOD ROAD

RICHMOND

CHURCH STREET

Church St Bridge

CHAPEL ST

South Yarra Railw. Bridge

RAILWAY

PRAHRAN

Life Belt

Richmond Boat Sheds

Botanical Gardens Bridge

ANDERSON ST

BOTANICAL GARDENS

Old Pumping House

Pumping House, Well & Tank

FITZROY

JOHNSTON ST

VICTORIA PARADE

HODDLE STREET

SOUTH YARRA

MELBOURNE

SWANSTON ST

COLLINS ST

FLINDERS ST

11 10 9 8 7 6 5 4 3 2 1

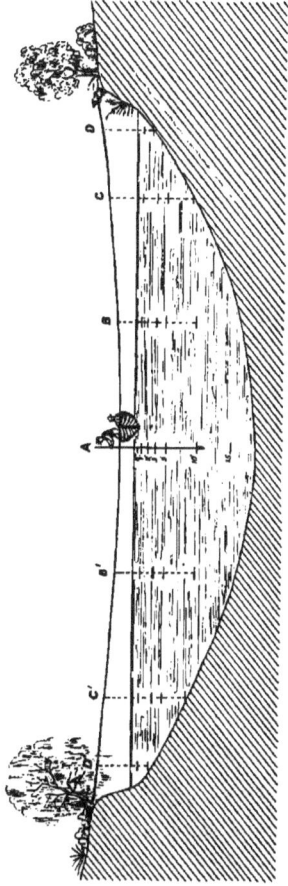

TABLE I.

CHLORINE contained in Yarra Water at Site of present Pumping House (Represented in parts per 100,000).

DECEMBER. | **JANUARY.**

Well.
Surface
6 inches deep
1 foot
1 feet

Tank.
Surface
6 inches deep
1 foot
1 feet

D´. 3 feet off the Left Bank.
Surface
1 foot deep
Bottom (about 4 feet)

C´. 13 feet off the Left Bank.
Surface
1 foot deep
2 feet
Bottom (about 8 feet)

B´. About 20 feet Left of Mid-stream.
Surface
6 inches deep
1 foot
2 feet
10 ,,

A. Mid-stream.
Surface
6 inches deep
1 foot
2 feet
4 ,,
5 ,,
10 ,,
15 ,,

TABLE I.

CHLORINE contained in Yarra Water at Site of present Pumping House—continued.

	DECEMBER.									JANUARY.																					
	11th	16th a.m.	16th p.m.	18th p.m.	14th a.m.	18th a.m.	10th a.m.	31st a.m.	2nd	9th a.m.	9th p.m.	16th a.m.	16th p.m.	17th a.m./p.m.	18th	19th a.m.	20th a.m.	21st a.m./p.m.	22nd a.m./p.m.	23rd a.m.	23rd p.m.	24th a.m./p.m.	25th a.m.	28th a.m./p.m.	29th a.m./p.m.	30th a.m.	30th p.m. a.m./p.m.	31st p.m.
B. About 10 feet off Right of Mid-stream.																												
Surface				2·5				48·5	39·75	19·25																		
6 inches deep				2·5			41·3	39·75	18·75																			
1 foot				2·5			45·0	39·0	18·75																			
2 feet				2·5			47·0	39·75	19·75																			
3 "				2·5			44·5	39·0	19·0																			
10 "							75·0	63·0	18·0																			
C. 13 feet off the Right Bank.																												
Surface				2·5			49·0	44·5	21·0																			
1 foot deep				2·5			49·5	46·5	21·0																			
2 feet				2·5			49·5	46·5	21·0																			
3 feet				2·5			50·5	50·0	20·5																			
Bottom (about 8 feet)							80·0	38·0	98·0																			
D. 3 feet off the Right Bank.																												
Surface				2·5			51·5	19·7	20·0		11·0									12·75	12·75					19·0		
1 foot deep				2·5			51·0	50·0	20·1		11·0							41·190		41·190	12·125					121·190		
Bottom (about 4 feet)							51·0	50·0	20·0		11·0							41·150		41·150						41·150		

NOTES.—H. signifies High Tide; L, Low Tide.——(a) 1·16 inches rain fell at Melbourne Observatory on 21st to 23rd December.——(b) ·09 inches rain fell at Melbourne Observatory on 7th January.——(c) ·91 inches rain fell at Melbourne Observatory on 11th January.

TABLE 1.

CHLORINE contained in Yarra Water at Site of present Pumping House—*continued.*

TABLE I.

CHLORINE contained in Yarra Water at Site of present Pumping House—*continued.*

	FEBRUARY.																				MARCH.							
	1st	3rd	4th	5th	6th	7th	8th	10th	11th	11th	13th	14th 15th	17th	18th	19th 20th	21st	22nd	24th	25th 26th	4th	7th	11th 14th 18th 25th 28th

B. About 10 feet Right of Mid-stream.

Surface
6 inches deep
1 foot
2 feet
10 ,, ,,

C. 13 feet off the Right Bank.

Surface
1 foot deep
2 feet ,, ,,
Bottom (about 8 feet)

D. 3 feet off the Right Bank.

Surface
1 foot deep
Bottom (about 4 feet)

Tides Half Way.   *Tides Half Way.*   *Tides Half Way.*

NOTE.—H, signifies High Tide; L, Low Tide.——(a) ·20 inches of rain fell at Melbourne Observatory on 7th March.——(c) ·10 inches of rain fell at Melbourne Observatory on 17th February.——(e) ·12 rain fell at Melbourne Observatory on 7th March.——(g) ·15 inches rain fell at Melbourne Observatory on 11th March.——(b) ·67 inches rain fell at Melbourne Observatory from 19th to 21st March.

TABLE II.

Chlorine in Yarra, near Old Pumping House. (Represented in parts per 100,000.)

	December 18th p.m. L.	December 24th a.m. L.	January 2nd a.m. H.	January 9th p.m. L.	January 9th a.m. L.	January 16th p.m. H.	January 16th a.m. H.	January 16th p.m. L.	January 23rd a.m. L.	January 23rd p.m. H.	January 30th a.m. H.	January 30th p.m. L.	February 6th a.m. L.
D'. 3 feet off the Left Bank.													
Surface	...	2·3	17·2	37·0	36·0	13·5	29·5	39·0	111·0	69·5	86·0	137·0	119·0
1 foot deep	...	2·3	18·4	36·5	36·25	13·5	24·5	38·5	...	...	...	...	...
2 feet „	...	...	...	...	...	...	...	...	112·0	69·5	86·5	142·0	122·0
Bottom (about 4 feet deep)	...	2·3	18·4	37·5	36·25	14·5	26·0	38·5	70·5	...	...	...	124·0
C'. 13 feet off the Left Bank.													
Surface	...	2·3	...	...	...	...	...	...	...	...	...	...	...
1 foot deep	...	2·3	...	...	...	...	...	...	...	...	...	...	...
2 feet „	...	2·3	...	...	...	...	...	...	...	...	...	...	...
3 „ „	...	2·3	...	...	...	...	...	...	...	...	...	...	...
Bottom (from 6 to 8 feet deep)	...	2·3	...	...	...	...	...	...	...	...	...	...	...
B'. About 20 feet left of Mid-stream.													
Surface	...	2·3	...	...	...	...	...	...	...	...	...	...	...
6 inches deep	...	2·3	...	...	...	...	...	...	...	...	...	...	...
1 foot „	...	2·3	...	...	...	...	...	...	...	...	...	...	...
2 feet „	...	2·3	...	...	...	...	...	...	...	...	...	...	...
3 „ „	...	2·3	...	...	...	...	...	...	...	...	...	...	...
10 „ „	...	2·4	...	...	...	...	...	...	...	...	...	...	...
A. Mid-stream.													
Surface	30·6	2·2	16·6	34·0	29·0	14·0	18·5	34·0	77·0	70·75	87·5	123·5	126·0
6 inches deep	36·8	2·2	...	...	...	...	...	...	...	...	...	...	...
1 foot „	38·4	2·3	22·2	36·5	29·0	14·0	22·5	34·25	135·0	63·75	96·0	129·0	130·5
2 feet „	...	2·3	...	...	...	...	...	...	...	...	...	...	...
3 „ „	40·8	2·4	...	...	...	...	...	...	84·5	74·75	112·0	135·0	136·5
4 „ „	...	...	...	...	...	...	...	...	...	...	...	...	...
5 „ „	...	2·3	...	...	...	...	...	...	...	...	...	...	...
10 „ „	363·0	2·3	...	...	...	...	...	...	...	...	...	...	...
15 „ „	...	2·3	763·0	980·0	876·0	227·0	946·0	993·0	3,275·0	1,262·5	1,120·0	1,365·0	1,400·0
B. About 20 feet right of Mid-stream.													
Surface	...	2·3	...	...	...	...	...	...	...	...	...	...	...
6 inches deep	...	2·3	...	...	...	...	...	...	...	...	...	...	...
1 foot „	...	2·3	...	...	...	...	...	...	...	...	...	...	...
2 feet „	...	2·3	...	...	...	...	...	...	...	...	...	...	...
3 „ „	...	2·3	...	...	...	...	...	...	...	...	...	...	...
10 „ „	...	2·3	...	...	...	...	...	...	...	...	...	...	...
C. 13 feet off Right Bank.													
Surface	...	2·3	...	...	...	...	...	...	...	...	...	...	...
1 foot deep	...	2·3	...	...	...	...	...	...	...	...	...	...	...
2 feet „	...	2·3	...	...	...	...	...	...	...	...	...	...	...
3 „ „	...	2·3	...	...	...	...	...	...	...	...	...	...	...
Bottom (from 6 to 8 feet deep)	...	2·3	...	...	...	...	...	...	...	...	...	...	...
D. 3 feet off Right Bank.													
Surface	...	2·2	25·0	46·0	25·5	15·5	21·5	44·0	65·0	77·5	100·0	119·0	130·0
1 foot deep	...	2·3	26·4	46·0	25·5	16·0	21·5	44·0	...	...	...	...	...
2 feet „	...	...	...	...	...	...	...	...	109·5	77·5	101·0	124·5	130·0
Bottom (about 4 feet deep)	...	...	40·4	46·0	25·5	17·0	22·5	44·0	69·0	79·0	119·0	...	...

H. signifies High Tide.
L. „ Low „

TABLE III.

CHLORINE in Yarra Water, a little below Botanic Gardens Footbridge. (In parts per 100,000.)

—	December 18th p.m. L	December 24th a.m. L	January 2nd a.m. H	2nd p.m. L	9th a.m. L	9th p.m. H	16th a.m. H	16th p.m. L	21st a.m. L	21st p.m. H	22nd a.m. L	22nd p.m. H	23rd a.m. L	23rd p.m. H
D′. 3 feet off Left Bank.														
Surface	..	2·2	17.4	36·5	29·5	14·25	31·5	29·5	61·25	72·0	78·75	92·5	92·0	64·5
1 foot deep	..	2·2	17·2	36·5	29·5	14·25	32·0	28·0	..	..	..	..	..	..
2 feet "	..	..	..	..	..	..	..	..	..	..	..	..	92·5	64·0
Bottom (about 4 feet deep)	..	2·2	18·0	36·5	32·5	14·25	38·5	30·0	61·0	76·0	78·75	94·0	..	..
C′. 13 feet off Left Bank.														
Surface	..	2·2	..	..	..	..	37·5	28·25	..	..	..	..	90·5	68·5
1 foot deep	..	2·2	..	..	..	..	38·0	28·25	..	..	..	..	..	..
2 feet "	..	2·2	..	..	..	..	38·0	30·75	..	..	..	..	91·5	66·5
3 " "	..	2·2	..	..	..	..	42·0	34·0	..	..	..	..	..	..
4 " "	..	..	..	..	..	..	..	..	..	..	..	..	91·5	63·5
6 " "	..	..	..	..	..	..	..	..	..	..	..	..	91·5	57·0
Bottom (about 8 feet deep)	..	2·4	..	..	..	..	74·5	290·0	..	..	..	..	..	..
B′. About 20 feet left of Mid-stream.														
Surface	..	2·2	..	..	..	..	17·75	26·0	..	..	..	..	85·75	69·5
6 inches deep	..	2·2	..	..	..	..	20·5	24·5	..	..	..	..	..	..
1 foot "	..	2·2	..	..	..	..	21·5	21·25	..	..	..	..	..	..
2 feet "	..	2·2	..	..	..	..	24·5	20·75	..	..	..	..	94·0	69·0
3 " "	..	2·2	..	..	..	..	27·75	21·5	..	..	..	..	..	..
4 " "	..	..	..	..	..	..	..	..	..	..	..	..	92·0	74·0
5 " "	..	..	..	..	..	..	..	..	..	..	..	..	..	..
6 " "	..	..	..	..	..	..	..	..	..	..	..	..	270·0	107·0
9 " "	..	..	..	..	..	..	..	..	..	..	..	..	1,090·0	109·0
10 " "	..	3·0	..	..	..	..	683·0	691·5	..	..	..	..	..	..
12 " "	..	..	..	..	..	..	..	..	..	..	..	..	..	..
15 " "	..	..	..	..	..	..	..	..	..	..	..	..	..	..
A. Mid-stream.														
Surface	21·2	2·4	8·2	24·5	10·0	8·5	18·5	19·5	..	..	..	..	76·5	67
6 inches deep	21·4	2·4	..	..	..	..	18·0	21·0	50·0	27·2	65·5	62·5	..	..
1 foot "	21·2	2·4	8·4	25·5	13·0	8·5	19·0	21·0	..	..	..	..	..	..
1½ feet "	..	..	..	..	..	..	..	..	..	..	66·25	67·15	..	..
2 " "	..	2·4	..	..	..	..	21·5	21·5	..	..	..	..	87·5	71·25
3 " "	23·4	2·4	..	..	..	..	24·0	25·5	56·75	51·5	68·75	67·0	..	..
4 " "	..	..	..	..	..	..	..	..	..	..	..	..	93·0	72·5
5 " "	..	2·4	..	..	..	..	60·5	30·5	..	..	..	..	..	..
6 " "	..	..	..	..	..	..	..	..	..	..	..	..	111·0	142·5
9 " "	..	..	..	..	..	..	..	..	..	..	..	..	108·0	1,025·0
10 " "	610·0	2·2	..	..	..	..	796·0	612·0	..	..	..	..	..	..
12 " "	..	..	..	..	..	..	..	..	..	..	..	..	1,240·0	1,275·0
15 " "	..	2·2	807·0	602·0	738·0	774·0	875·0	996·0	..	..	..	..	1,267·5	1,315·0

—	January 24th a.m. L	24th p.m. H	25th a.m. L	28th a.m. L	28th p.m. H	29th a.m. H	29th p.m. L	30th a.m. H	30th p.m. L	31st a.m. H	31st p.m. L
D′. 3 feet off Left Bank.											
Surface	80·0	122·0	126	186	110	92·0	75·25	96·0	131·0	52	86·0
1 foot deep	..	..	..	..	..	..	..	..	..	..	..
2 feet "	..	..	..	..	..	..	..	109·0	131·0	..	..
Bottom (about 4 feet deep)	84·25	121·0	127	196	112	92·0	75·25	105·0	..	54	84·5
C′. 13 feet off Left Bank.											
Surface	..	..	..	..	..	..	..	94·0	146·0	..	..
1 foot deep	..	..	..	..	..	..	..	..	..	..	..
2 feet "	..	..	..	..	..	..	..	103·0	137·0	..	..
3 " "	..	..	..	..	..	..	..	..	..	..	..
4 " "	..	..	..	..	..	..	..	111·0	137·0	..	..
6 " "	..	..	..	..	..	..	..	113·5	173·5	..	..
Bottom (about 8 feet deep)	..	..	..	..	..	..	..	822·5	987·0	..	..
B′. About 20 feet left of Mid-stream.											
Surface	..	..	..	..	..	..	..	78·0	112·0	..	..
6 inches deep	..	..	..	..	..	..	..	..	..	..	..
1 foot "	..	..	..	..	..	..	..	..	..	..	..
2 feet "	..	..	..	..	..	..	..	80·0	117·5	..	..
3 " "	..	..	..	..	..	..	..	..	..	..	..
4 " "	..	..	..	..	..	..	..	94·0	115·0	..	..
5 " "	..	..	..	..	..	..	..	..	..	..	..
6 " "	..	..	..	..	..	..	..	120·0	124·5	..	..
9 " "	..	..	..	..	..	..	..	810·0	107·0	..	..
10 " "	..	..	..	..	..	..	..	..	..	..	..
12 " "	..	..	..	..	..	..	..	1,170·0	1,295·0	..	..
15 " "	..	..	..	..	..	..	..	1,180·0	1,295·0	..	..
A. Mid-stream.											
Surface	68·0	99·0	99	161	109	83·0	64·0	84·0	107·0	37	71·5
6 inches deep	..	..	..	..	..	..	..	..	..	..	..
1 foot "	..	..	..	..	..	..	..	..	..	..	..
1½ feet "	70·0	102·0	100	162	111	113·5	64·0	..	..	39	71·0
2 " "	..	..	..	..	..	..	..	80·7	114·0	..	..
3 " "	75·5	110·5	111	169	109	112·5	64·75	..	..	36	72·5
4 " "	..	..	..	..	..	..	..	86·5	120·0	..	..
5 " "	..	..	..	..	..	..	..	..	..	..	..
6 " "	..	..	..	..	..	..	..	121·0	124·0	..	..
9 " "	..	..	..	..	..	..	..	787·5	519·0	..	..
10 " "	..	..	..	..	..	..	..	..	..	..	..
12 " "	..	..	..	..	..	..	..	1,150·0	1,175·0	..	..
15 " "	..	..	..	..	..	..	..	1,230·0	1,190·0	..	..

—	February 1st a.m. H	3rd a.m. H	3rd p.m. L	4th a.m. L	4th p.m. H	5th a.m. L	5th p.m. H	6th a.m. L	6th p.m. H	7th a.m. L	7th p.m. H	8th p.m. L	10th p.m. H
D′. 3 feet off Left Bank.													
Surface	39	45·5	111	88·5	61·0	89	73	147·0	90·0	103·0	38·5	160·5	15·9
1 foot deep	..	..	..	..	..	..	..	..	..	..	..	..	..
2 feet "	..	..	..	..	..	..	..	131·0	..	..	..	..	..
Bottom (about 4 feet deep)	19	70·0	125	90·0	67·0	96	72	124·0	90·0	108·0	56·0	160·5	19·5
C′. 13 feet off Left Bank.													
Surface	..	..	..	..	..	..	..	123·0	..	..	..	..	..
1 foot deep	..	..	..	..	..	..	..	..	..	..	..	..	..
2 feet "	..	..	..	..	..	..	..	126·0	..	..	..	..	..
3 " "	..	..	..	..	..	..	..	..	..	..	..	..	..
4 " "	..	..	..	..	..	..	..	106·0	..	..	..	..	..
6 " "	..	..	..	..	..	..	..	118·2	..	..	..	..	..
Bottom (about 8 feet deep)	..	..	..	..	..	..	..	..	..	..	..	..	..
B′. About 20 feet left of Mid-stream.													
Surface	..	..	..	..	..	..	..	105·0	..	..	..	..	..
6 inches deep	..	..	..	..	..	..	..	..	..	..	..	..	..
1 foot "	..	..	..	..	..	..	..	..	..	..	..	..	..
2 feet "	..	..	..	..	..	..	..	114·0	..	..	..	..	..
3 " "	..	..	..	..	..	..	..	..	..	..	..	..	..
4 " "	..	..	..	..	..	..	..	127·0	..	..	..	..	..
5 " "	..	..	..	..	..	..	..	..	..	..	..	..	..
6 " "	..	..	..	..	..	..	..	167·0	..	..	..	..	..
9 " "	..	..	..	..	..	..	..	1,255·0	..	..	..	..	..
10 " "	..	..	..	..	..	..	..	..	..	..	..	..	..
12 " "	..	..	..	..	..	..	..	1,265·0	..	..	..	..	..
15 " "	..	..	..	..	..	..	..	1,305·0	..	..	..	..	..
A. Mid-stream.													
Surface	..	75·0	105	69·5	41·0	78	53	113·0	70·5	81·0	72·0	126·25	72
6 inches deep	..	..	..	..	..	..	..	..	..	..	..	..	..
1 foot "	..	..	..	..	..	..	..	..	..	..	..	..	..
1½ feet "	19	59·0	106	71·5	48·5	86	55	..	..	..	..	..	..
2 " "	..	..	..	..	..	..	..	114·0	..	..	..	..	..
3 " "	49	61·5	116	83·0	48·0	89	57	..	89·5	113·0	70·5	137·0	13·8
4 " "	..	..	..	..	..	..	..	133·0	..	..	..	..	..
5 " "	..	..	..	..	..	..	..	..	..	..	..	..	..
6 " "	..	..	..	..	..	..	..	567·0	..	..	..	..	..
9 " "	..	..	..	..	..	..	..	965·0	..	..	..	..	..
10 " "	..	..	..	..	..	..	..	..	..	..	..	..	..
12 " "	..	..	..	..	..	..	..	1,300·0	..	..	..	..	..
15 " "	..	..	..	..	..	..	..	1,315·0	..	..	..	..	..

B. About 20 feet right of Mid-stream.

Surface
6 inches deep
1 foot
2 feet
3 "
4 "
6 "
9 "
12 "
15 "

C. 15 feet off Right Bank.

Surface
1 foot deep
2 feet
3 "
4 "
Bottom (about 8 feet deep)

D. 3 feet off Right Bank.

Surface
1 foot deep
2 feet
Bottom (about 4 feet deep)

TABLE IV.

Chlorine contained in Yarra Water, at Site near Richmond Boat Sheds (in Parts per 100,000).

Upper section — JANUARY / FEBRUARY

	22nd a.m. L	23rd a.m. L	23rd p.m. H	14th a.m. L	14th p.m. H	15th a.m. L	18th a.m. L	13th a.m. H	29th p.m. L	30th a.m. L	30th p.m. H	31st a.m. H	31st p.m. L	1st a.m. H	2nd p.m. H	3rd p.m. L	4th a.m. L	4th p.m. H	5th a.m. L	5th p.m. H	6th a.m. L	6th p.m. H	7th a.m. L	7th p.m. H
IV. 3 feet off Left Bank.																								
Surface	59·0	68·5	51·5	63·75	87·5	93·0	139	67·5	57·0	60·0	99	28	62·0	25	38	105	66·0	39·5	73·0	53	80	71	77	71·5
2 feet deep	60·5	69·0	51·0	66·25	86·5	98·25	137	67·0	59·5	61·0	93	35	62·0	25	38	113	67·0	39·5	80·0	57	80	70	77	61·5
3 ,,			51·0							61·0	99	35		25					79		79			
4 ,,											99										490			
A. Mid-stream.																								
Surface	52·5	52·25	46·0	55·5	74·5	88·75	127	39·5	55·0	52·5	89	33	60·0	14	50	123	68·5	36·5	66·5	49	72	57	71	56·5
2 feet deep	57·5	57·0	47·0	67·5	82·0	97·5	138	64·0	56·0	54·0	92	38	61·5	14	55	125	83·0	36·0	70·5	49	73	63	75	61·75
3 ,,		68·5	47·5						57·0	96											99			
4 ,,	3,150·0	3,150·0	1,145·0						655·0	1,005											490			
15 ,,																								
D. 3 feet off Right Bank.																								
Surface		69·5	41·5								99										99			
2 feet deep		71·5	43·5								96													
			49·0																					

Lower section — FEBRUARY / MARCH (Half Tides in March)

	8th p.m. L	10th a.m. L	10th p.m. H	11th a.m. L	11th p.m. H	12th a.m. H	12th p.m. L	13th a.m. H	13th p.m. L	14th a.m. H	15th a.m. L	17th p.m. H	18th p.m. L	19th p.m. H	1st a.m. H	2nd p.m. H	5th p.m. L	6th a.m. L	7th a.m. L	11th p.m. H	14th a.m. L	15th a.m. L	16th a.m. L	18th p.m. H
IV. 3 feet off Left Bank.																								
Surface	109·5	190	153	160	118·0	124	190·5	93·5	126·0	(a) 83·0	67·5	(b) 8·5	7·0	6·0	10·0	6·5	91	109·5	(c) 91	(d) 130	168	(e) 14	106·5	
2 feet deep	110·0	190	161	160	117·0	130	130·0	92·5	126·0	89·0	68·0	9·5	8·5	8·2	10·0	7·0	93	113·5	93	140	180	34	118·0	
3 ,,																								
4 ,,																								
A. Mid-stream.																								
Surface	102·0	163	154	143	114·5	108	130·0	80·0	95·5	72·5	56·5	7·0	7·5	4·6	6·5	86	95·0	86	145	163	138·5	26	116·5	
2 feet deep	108·5	165	164	146	116·5	122	133·0	93·0	112·5	77·5	57·5	8·0	7·0	4·8	7·0	92	106·0	83	151	163	144·0	31	115·0	
3 ,,															7·0									
4 ,,																								
15 ,,																								
D. 3 feet off Right Bank.																								
Surface																								
2 feet deep																								
4 ,,																								

NOTE.—(a) ·20 inches rain fell at Melbourne Observatory on the 14th February.—(b) ·20 inches rain fell at Melbourne Observatory on the 17th February.—(c) ·12 inches rain fell at Melbourne Observatory on 7th March.—(d) ·15 inches rain fell at Melbourne Observatory on 11th March.—(e) ·07 inches rain fell at Melbourne Observatory on 19th to 21st March.

TABLE V.

CHLORINE contained at Sites Nos. 5–13.

	FEBRUARY																	MARCH							
	6th	7th	7th	8th	10th	10th	11th	11th	11th	11th	13th	13th	14th	15th	17th	18th	19th	16th (Half Tides)	4th	7th	11th	14th	18th	25th	28th
	p.m. H	a.m. L	p.m. H	p.m. L	a.m. L	p.m. H	p.m. L	p.m. H	a.m. L	p.m. L	a.m. H	p.m. L	a.m. H	a.m. H	p.m. H	p.m. H	p.m. H	a.m. H	(c)	(c)	(c)		(e)	(e)	(e)
No. 5. Life-belt. Left bank—Surface	…	…	…	…	…	…	…	…	…	…	…	…	…	…	…	…	…	…	…	…	…	…	…	…	…
„ 3 feet deep	…	…	…	…	…	…	…	…	…	…	…	…	…	…	…	…	…	…	…	…	…	…	…	…	…
Mid-stream—Surface	…	…	…	…	…	…	…	…	…	…	…	…	…	…	…	…	…	…	…	…	…	…	…	…	…
„ 3 feet deep	…	…	…	…	…	…	…	…	…	…	…	…	…	…	…	…	…	…	…	…	…	…	…	…	…
No. 6. South Yarra Bridge. Left bank—Surface	…	…	…	…	…	…	…	…	…	…	…	…	…	…	…	…	…	…	…	…	…	…	…	…	…
„ 3 feet deep	…	…	…	…	…	…	…	…	…	…	…	…	…	…	…	…	…	…	…	…	…	…	…	…	…
Mid-stream—Surface	…	…	…	…	…	…	…	…	…	…	…	…	…	…	…	…	…	…	…	…	…	…	…	…	…
„ 3 feet deep	…	…	…	…	…	…	…	…	…	…	…	…	…	…	…	…	…	…	…	…	…	…	…	…	…
No. 7. Church-street Bridge. Left bank—Surface	…	…	…	…	…	…	…	…	…	…	…	…	…	…	…	…	…	…	…	…	…	…	…	…	…
„ 3 feet deep	…	…	…	…	…	…	…	…	…	…	…	…	…	…	…	…	…	…	…	…	…	…	…	…	…
Mid-stream—Surface	…	…	…	…	…	…	…	…	…	…	…	…	…	…	…	…	…	…	…	…	…	…	…	…	…
„ 3 feet deep	…	…	…	…	…	…	…	…	…	…	…	…	…	…	…	…	…	…	…	…	…	…	…	…	…
No. 8. Quarry Bend. Left bank—Surface	…	…	…	…	…	…	…	…	…	…	…	…	…	…	…	…	…	…	…	…	…	…	…	…	…
„ 3 feet deep	…	…	…	…	…	…	…	…	…	…	…	…	…	…	…	…	…	…	…	…	…	…	…	…	…
Mid-stream—Surface	…	…	…	…	…	…	…	…	…	…	…	…	…	…	…	…	…	…	…	…	…	…	…	…	…
„ 3 feet deep	…	…	…	…	…	…	…	…	…	…	…	…	…	…	…	…	…	…	…	…	…	…	…	…	…
No. 9. Entrance to Toorak Bend. Mid-stream—Surface	—	…	…	…	…	…	…	…	…	…	…	…	…	…	…	…	…	…	…	…	…	…	…	…	…
No. 10. Toorak Bend. Left bank—Surface	…	…	…	…	…	…	…	…	…	…	…	…	…	…	…	…	…	…	…	…	…	…	…	…	…
„ 3 feet deep	…	…	…	…	…	…	…	…	…	…	…	…	…	…	…	…	…	…	…	…	…	…	…	…	…
Mid-stream—Surface	…	…	…	…	…	…	…	…	…	…	…	…	…	…	…	…	…	…	…	…	…	…	…	…	…
„ 3 feet deep	…	…	…	…	…	…	…	…	…	…	…	…	…	…	…	…	…	…	…	…	…	…	…	…	…
No. 11. Below Twickenham Ferry. Left bank—Surface	…	…	…	…	…	…	…	…	…	…	…	…	…	…	…	…	…	…	…	…	…	…	…	…	…
„ 3 feet deep	…	…	…	…	…	…	…	…	…	…	…	…	…	…	…	…	…	…	…	…	…	…	…	…	…
Mid-stream—Surface	…	…	…	…	…	…	…	…	…	…	…	…	…	…	…	…	…	…	…	…	…	…	…	…	…
„ 3 feet deep	…	…	…	…	…	…	…	…	…	…	…	…	…	…	…	…	…	…	…	…	…	…	…	…	…
No. 12. Below Dight's Falls. Left bank—Surface	…	…	…	…	…	…	…	…	…	…	…	…	…	…	…	…	…	…	…	…	…	…	…	…	…
„ 3 feet deep	…	…	…	…	…	…	…	…	…	…	…	…	…	…	…	…	…	…	…	…	…	…	…	…	…
No. 13. Above Dight's Falls. Left bank—Surface	…	…	…	…	…	…	…	…	…	…	…	…	…	…	…	…	…	…	…	…	…	…	…	…	…
„ 3 feet deep	…	…	…	…	…	…	…	…	…	…	…	…	…	…	…	…	…	…	…	…	…	…	…	…	…

(a) 1·20 inches rain fell at Melbourne Observatory on the 14th February.—(b) 1·20 inches rain fell at Melbourne Observatory on the 17th February.—(c) ·70 inches rain fell at Melbourne Observatory on 7th March.—(d) ·15 inches rain fell at Melbourne Observatory on 11th March.—(e) ·67 inches rain fell at Melbourne Observatory on 19th March to 21st March.

TABLE VI.

Monthly and Yearly Rainfall at Melbourne for Years 1856–90.

--	January.	February.	March.	April.	May.	June.	July.	August.	September.	October.	November.	December.	Total.
1856	2·38	0·98	2·82	4·76	2·96	2·99	2·35	1·22	3·49	2·78	1·39	1·84	29·76
1857	1·23	3·98	3·80	0·99	2·00	1·99	1·16	1·69	3·83	5·28	2·12	0·83	28·90
1858	0·88	4·91	1·09	0·60	1·38	0·76	2·07	1·62	2·17	0·87	3·19	6·47	26·01
1859	2·86	0·83	0·18	1·29	3·32	4·51	1·04	0·95	2·77	2·33	1·71	1·03	22·82
1860	1·97	1·08	0·96	4·53	0·99	1·72	1·21	0·79	2·72	1·97	2·38	5·06	25·38
1861	2·25	4·62	2·65	1·29	0·84	1·78	2·14	1·47	3·19	4·39	1·46	2·58	29·16
1862	1·25	0·19	1·08	3·56	4·31	2·99	2·26	1·95	0·98	2·03	0·32	1·16	22·08
1863	1·84	2·74	3·84	1·76	2·54	1·16	2·87	2·10	1·99	4·89	3·51	7·18	36·42
1864	2·07	2·63	1·80	4·53	1·02	0·81	2·83	2·50	2·28	4·08	0·64	2·21	27·40
1865	0·16	0·59	1·26	0·72	3·41	1·64	2·05	1·22	1·87	0·78	0·89	1·35	15·94
1866	1·43	0·35	2·14	0·57	2·92	1·64	2·04	2·26	2·08	3·25	2·17	1·56	22·41
1867	1·92	2·68	0·75	2·42	2·38	1·80	1·66	1·91	3·43	3·35	0·87	3·34	25·79
1868	2·11	0·99	1·02	1.44	1·48	1·21	1·46	1·01	2·13	1·05	3·19	1·18	18·27
1869	1·46	0·89	1·53	1·27	1·99	2·37	1·13	1·65	1·58	7·61	2·12	0·98	24·58
1870	3·15	0·03	0·34	4·88	2·78	3·32	3·16	2·14	5·87	4·38	3·23	0·49	33·77
1871	3·00	3·23	2·37	1·29	1·39	1·25	2·08	3·58	1·86	2·88	4·19	3·05	30·17
1872	4·98	0·99	1·82	1·50	2·43	3·66	2·17	2·83	1·31	2·86	4·50	3·47	32·52
1873	2·07	4·67	1·84	2·07	1·31	2·69	1·40	2·07	2·57	2·92	1·41	0·59	25·61
1874	2·14	0·88	6·36	1·71	2·07	1·45	1·86	1·95	2·84	2·80	2·12	1·92	28·10
1875	0·57	5·42	0·86	4·68	2·91	2·82	1·92	2·28	1·56	3·18	2·78	3·89	32·87
1876	1·40	0·49	2·67	2·40	2·28	1·20	1 05	1·86	1·64	2·64	5·02	1·40	24·05
1877	0·28	3·10	3·16	4·56	3·42	0·73	1·41	1·08	2·62	1·26	0·86	1·62	24·10
1878	0·04	4·34	5·85	2·95	0·76	2·82	1·11	2·60	2·20	1·43	1·02	0·24	25·36
1879	1·11	0·94	0·43	1·49	2·11	1·14	1·28	1·47	1·84	3·23	2·47	1·67	19·28
1880	1·22	1·95	3·87	3·11	2·74	2·79	0·65	2·05	5·50	2·24	1·23	1·13	28·48
1881	0·75	0·29	2·43	1·20	1·68	2·24	0·68	2·97	0 61	3·05	5·05	3·13	24·08
1882	0·29	0·29	0 94	2·31	2·55	1·37	2·25	2·11	1·30	2·05	3·81	3·13	22·40
1883	0·42	1·57	4 15	0·95	1·99	1·96	2·55	0·87	1·64	2·79	3·22	1·60	23·71
1884	4·75	1·95	3·11	0·76	2·15	0·84	0·78	1·63	0·68	3·04	3·11	3·05	25·85
1885	0·75	2·74	2·39	2·52	1·23	3·63	1·13	1·56	3·93	1·99	3·54	1·53	26·94
1886	4·54	1·54	1·72	0·95	0·80	0·81	0·84	2·45	1·30	2·84	2·67	3·54	24·00
1887	1·11	2·67	0·78	4·84	1·98	3·04	2 68	0·96	2·71	2·83	3·66	5·13	32·39
1888	2·59	0·42	2·16	0 83	3 77	1·19	1·51	0·99	1·28	1·35	0·62	2·72	19·42
1889	4·22	1·50	0·24	3·60	0·94	2·78	1·64	2·06	1·51	2·86	4 27	1·52	27·14
1890	1·37	0·56	1·62										

TABLE VII.

Daily Rainfall at Melbourne Observatory for Years 1887–90.

* Rainfall for December, 1889, and January to March, 1890, taken from the reports as published in the *Argus*.

www.ingramcontent.com/pod-product-compliance
Lightning Source LLC
Chambersburg PA
CBHW031157090426
42738CB00008B/1374